CCSS Genre Fairy Tale

Essential Question
What can you do to get the information you need?

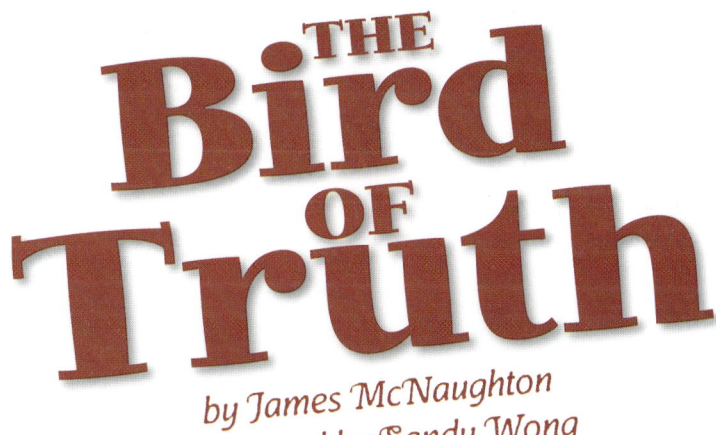

The Bird of Truth

by James McNaughton
illustrated by Sandy Wong

Chapter 1
Twins 2

Chapter 2
The Swallows 5

Chapter 3
The Bird of Truth 8

Chapter 4
Together Again. 13

Respond to Reading 16

PAIRED READ The Singers of Bremen 17

Focus on Genre 20

CHAPTER 1
TWINS

One day, a fisherman saw something floating on the river. It sparkled in the sun.

It was a cradle made of crystal! He lifted it from the water, and inside were twin babies, a girl and a boy.

The man took the babies home to his wife, but when she saw them, she threw up her hands in **despair**. "We already have eight children!" she cried.

"I couldn't let them drift out to sea," replied her husband.

"You're right," she sighed. "Ten can eat as cheaply as eight."

The twins grew up to be good and gentle. Their adoptive parents came to love them even more than their own children. The other children were jealous and were mean to the twins.

To escape their teasing, the twins spent hours by the river. They fed the birds bread, and in return, the birds taught the children to speak their language.

The other children continued to tease and taunt the twins, even though the twins were kind to them. "You think you're better than us, but at least we have a mother and father. You've only got the river, like the toads and frogs," they said.

The **insult** made the twins realize that they could not stay. They decided to change their **circumstances**. The next morning, the twins set off to find their **destiny**.

STOP AND CHECK

How did the twins become part of the fisherman's family?

CHAPTER 2
THE SWALLOWS

The twins walked all day. When the children saw a house that evening, they imagined a hot meal and a comfortable bed. But their **expectations** were not met. The house was dark and deserted.

They tried to act brave. "At least we'll be able to sleep inside," said the boy.

His sister smiled. "Yes, we will decide what to do tomorrow."

They went inside and lay down. Some swallows flew in and **perched** on the beams overhead. Unaware that the children knew their language, they began to chat freely. The **presence** of the birds was comforting. The twins closed their eyes, relaxed, and listened.

"It is good to be back," said a swallow.

"It's good to have you back," called the others.

"Why did you leave the palace?" asked one.

"There were too many cats!" said the palace swallow.

"Tell us the palace news!" said another.

"Yes," cried the others. "Tell us!"

The palace swallow began.

"Many years ago, the king married a tailor's daughter. The nobles tried to prevent the marriage because they wanted the king to marry one of their daughters instead. Then the king went to war. When he returned, his wife was gone. The nobles told him the terrible news. The queen had given birth to twins but the babies died. As a result, the queen was so sad that she shut herself away in a tower."

"Was that true?" asked a country swallow.

"Of course not!" replied the palace swallow. "The nobles had put her in prison. They told the gardener to kill the babies, but he couldn't do it. Instead, he put the babies into the river in a crystal cradle. A fisherman found them."

STOP AND CHECK

What do the children learn from the swallows?

CHAPTER 3
THE BIRD OF TRUTH

"They're talking about us!" whispered the girl. Their adoptive parents told them they were found in a crystal cradle.

"Why don't the children return to the palace?" asked a country swallow.

"They can't prove who they are," said the palace swallow. "The king must **consult** the Bird of Truth, but she's trapped in a giant's castle with the Birds of Bad Faith."

The twins knew what they had to do.

The twins left to find the giant's castle the next morning. They walked and walked, but there was no sign of it. Then they noticed a turtledove in a tree above them.

"Please help us," the boy cried, using the bird's language. "We're looking for the castle where the Bird of Truth is trapped."

"Follow the wind," said the dove. "It is blowing toward the castle."

The twins followed the wind until they came to a large, dark castle. Its doors were wide open. The children hesitated. The children were **unsure** what to do next, so they hid behind an olive tree nearby.

"What shall we do?" the boy asked his sister.

"What shall you do?" repeated an owl who was sitting above them in the tree.

The twins leaped with joy. "We've come to free the Bird of Truth," said the boy. "How should we do it?"

"There is a large aviary inside," said the owl. "You'll see many brightly colored birds. Each one will tell you it is the Bird of Truth. Ignore them. They are the Birds of Bad Faith. Take only the small white bird. Go now! The giant is asleep."

The twins went in and quickly found the aviary. When they stepped inside, the birds all called out, claiming to be the Bird of Truth.

They ignored the **uproar** and looked around until they found a small white bird.

11

The girl reached out and picked up the Bird of Truth.

"Thank you. I have been waiting to be set free," the bird said.

The girl held the bird in her jacket. Then the twins ran as fast as they could.

The children were **terrified** that the giant would come after them. They ran until the castle was out of sight.

News that the Bird of Truth was free spread throughout the kingdom. The nobles were nervous. They were afraid the bird would **reveal** the truth to the king about the queen and the twins. So they sent eagles to hunt her.

> **STOP AND CHECK**
>
> Who helped the twins find the Bird of Truth? How?

CHAPTER 4
TOGETHER AGAIN

Finally, the king himself heard the rumor about the Bird of Truth being free. The king announced that whoever found the Bird of Truth must bring her to him.

So the twins headed for the palace. But the guards stopped them at the gates.

Suddenly, the Bird of Truth flew out of the girl's jacket and through a window into the king's chamber. "Your Majesty, I am the Bird of Truth," she said. "The children who brought me are outside the gates."

The king had the children brought to him and asked for an explanation.

So the Bird of Truth told the king about the nobles' plot.

Immediately, the king and the twins hurried to where the queen was imprisoned.

The queen was pale and sickly, but when she saw her husband and children, her face brightened.

"It's so good to see you," she said. "Why did you wait so long?"

The king was shocked. "I received a letter from you every month. Each letter told me to stay away."

"The nobles lied," she said. "I wrote to you every day and asked you to come."

The king hugged the queen and the children. "No one will ever separate us again!"

The king and his family returned to the city and were greeted by cheering crowds. A feast was held to celebrate. The fisherman and his wife were invited. The wicked nobles fled the kingdom and never returned. And so the royal family was **reunited** and lived happily ever after.

> **STOP AND CHECK**
>
> How are the twins reunited with their parents?

Respond to Reading

Summarize

Summarize the important events in *The Bird of Truth*. Your graphic organizer may help you.

Event	→	Outcomes
	→	
	→	
	→	
	→	

Text Evidence

1. How are the events in Chapter 2 similar to and different from the events in Chapter 3? **COMPARE AND CONTRAST**

2. What does the word *comforting* mean on page 5? Use clues in the next sentence to help you figure it out. **VOCABULARY**

3. Write about what happens to the twins. How do their lives change from the beginning to the end of the story? **WRITE ABOUT READING**

Genre **Fairy Tale**

Compare Texts
Read about talking animals who want new jobs.

The Singers of Bremen

There was once a donkey who carried sacks of flour from the mill. One day, the donkey overheard his master talking to another man. His master said the donkey was getting too old to work. After some **consideration**, the donkey decided to run away. He would find a job as a singer in the town of Bremen.

On the way to Bremen, the donkey met a dog who looked very sad. The dog had become too weak to hunt, and his master was going to replace him.

"Don't worry," said the donkey. "I'm going to Bremen to become a singer. You can come along."

On the way, they met a cat who was too tired to catch rats. Then they met a rooster who was about to be cooked for dinner. The cat and the rooster decided to become singers in Bremen, too.

By evening, the animals had not arrived in Bremen. They would have to sleep in the woods. The donkey and dog lay under a tree. The cat curled up on a branch. The rooster flew up to the top of a tree. He told the others he could see a light in the distance.

"Let's get a closer look," said the donkey. "We might find somewhere more comfortable to sleep."

They walked towards the light and soon came to a house. The donkey looked in the window and saw a gang of robbers eating a huge feast.

The animals talked and finally came up with a plan to get the robbers out of the house.

The donkey put his front hooves on the windowsill. The dog got up on the donkey's back. Then the cat jumped up on top of the dog. Finally, the rooster flew up and sat on the cat's head.

Then they began to sing. The donkey brayed, the dog howled, the cat yowled, and the rooster crowed. The robbers screamed and ran away in fright. They thought it was a monster.

The four friends went inside. They feasted like they hadn't eaten for a month. The robbers never returned. The four singers of Bremen were very comfortable in the house and decided to stay forever.

Make Connections

How did the animals find out what was happening in the house? **ESSENTIAL QUESTION**

Why do the characters in these two stories go on journeys? **TEXT TO TEXT**

Focus on Genre

Fairy Tales Usually, a character in a fairy tale must meet a challenge or find a way to reach a goal. People, animals, or magical creatures may help or trick the character along the way.

In a fairy tale, the good characters always win over the bad ones and live "happily ever after."

Read and Find In *The Bird of Truth*, the good twins are treated badly by the fisherman's children. The twins learn to talk to birds. This helps them to find out about their real parents. Their challenge is to find the Bird of Truth. She will tell the king what really happened after they were born.

The twins and their real parents live happily ever after.

Your Turn
With a partner, think of a fairy tale that you know, such as "Cinderella," or "The Princess and the Pea." Discuss the characters and the plot. Explain to the group why the story is a fairy tale.